PAIN-FREE GOLF

DR. CHRISTIAN REICHARDT, DC CCSP

WITH JON KLAGES

WWW.GOLF-HEALTH.COM

A GOLF-HEALTH PUBLICATION

© 2001

Fitness disclaimer

The health information presented in this book is intended as an educational resource only. It is not intended as a substitute for proper medical advice. If you have experienced pain for a long time or if your pain is of a severe nature, consult your chiropractic doctor, medical physician or physical therapist prior to utilizing this book. Discontinue any exercise that causes you severe discomfort or more pain. Neither the author nor the producer nor distributors of this information make any warranty of any kind in regard to the content of the information presented in this book.

How to Use This Book

Before we dive into the essence of Pain-Free Golf, I would like to make three things clear:

1 **This book will not teach you a new or better golf swing.**

2 **It will not interfere with your golf swing or your lessons; in fact, it will enhance what your pro has been trying to teach you and it will help you play better, consistently.**

3 **If you follow the evaluation and instructions in this book,** *you will play better golf.*

Golf tests your character, patience and determination, and therefore requires a good body as its base. The aim of *Pain-Free Golf* is to educate you about your body, and to show you how to overcome your body's physical restrictions so that you can play better golf.

Pain-Free Golf is for any handicap golfer whose body seems to get in the way of a successful golf swing. Written in an easy-to-follow manner, the book is filled with diagrams that clearly illustrate all the movements and exercises. You should be able to read through the entire book in about one hour, and the only equipment you need to have on hand is a golf club. (Any club will do.) The book's compact size makes it easy to carry. Once you have memorized your exercises, each workout session should only take a few minutes. You can do these exercises anywhere: your home, your office, on the golf course or on your vacation. Do them frequently and your game will improve dramatically.

The self-evaluation test will help you chart your progress, so retest yourself periodically. (Use a #2 pencil.) And show your golf pro the results – it will make him/her aware of your physical limitations, so your lessons can be custom tailored to you.

Last, but not least, remember: Go and have fun. Unless golf is your profession or livelihood, you don't need to approach it as work. Relax and enjoy your time on the course – ***Play golf; don't work golf.***

FOREWORD

I have played professional golf for 25 years. When I joined the LPGA TOUR in 1975, the mental side of golf was what we were taught to pay the most attention to – the physical aspects of it were secondary. Well, I am going to tell you that approach to the game has changed, and with that comes a lot of advice and many gurus.

Quite simply, it is common sense that if your body hurts, your brain's roadmap to your body is impaired–it may be not at this moment, this month or even this year, but like that bad hook shot that comes out of nowhere one day, you'll say, "What happened to me?"

I have been a longtime patient of Dr. Reichardt and I believe his exercises to increase agility are key to improving and maximizing your golf swing, both mentally and physically. Freeing your golf swing is his mantra, and I am all for that.

Golf has been my life's passion and if you take the time to read Dr. Reichardt's new book and follow his instructions, I believe your days on the links will be extended and more enjoyable and they will reward you with lower scores.

Sincerely,

Amy Alcott

OVERVIEW OF PAIN-FREE GOLF

CHAPTER 1

INTRODUCTION

INTRODUCTION

Pain – the sensation that makes whatever we are doing less fun. For golfers, pain – including soreness, aches or fatigue –can cloud an otherwise perfect day. We know that golf worsens the pain, but still we keep at it – hitting balls at the driving range or playing 18 holes with fast-paced, repetitive motions. All the while, the pain keeps growing, turning that cloud of discomfort into a full-fledged storm.

Well, you don't have to live with these clouds anymore. Imagine finishing a round of golf and feeling great. An exhilarating state . . . and one that is available to you.

Golfers go to great extremes to improve their game – buying the latest equipment and taking expensive lessons – only to experience aching muscles and persistent, nagging injuries. This happens because most golfers ignore the most important component behind successful golf and its enjoyment: the body.

Few of us have the natural ability of Tiger Woods or David Duval. But even they have to work at their bodies, several hours per day, in addition to their practice. Unfortunately, most golfers step up to the first tee, fling three or four clubs around them as a warm-up, and then fire their first shot at 85 to100 mph. No wonder they get hurt! Most of us wouldn't even approach a Saturday morning softball game without stretching, warming up, and making sure we drink plenty of water. But for some strange reason, we don't take the same personal care on the golf course.

As a golfer and a doctor who has treated amateur and professional athletes for the past 18 years, I was astonished to discover that there is no book on the market that deals with educating the golfer about the body. The few books on the shelves that are about exercise and golf are so complicated, it is difficult to follow the reasoning behind them.

The movement required in the golf swing places great demands on your body. The aim of *Pain-Free Golf* is to provide an easy-to-follow evaluation of your ability to perform the strenuous task of the "golf move." First, *Pain-Free Golf* will show you where you have restrictions within your body that prevent you from doing what your teacher or a book tells you to do. Then, it will give you ways to recognize and overcome these restrictions, allowing you to play a better, happier game of golf.

Pain-Free Golf is not intended as a replacement for golf lessons; on the contrary, by showing you where your body's restrictions are, the book will allow you and your golf pro to resume your lessons with a new understanding.

It's time to look at golf in a new way – from the perspective of our body, the incredible apparatus that enables us to propel a ball down the fairway at extraordinary speeds. Uncoiling at about a hundred mph, our body still lets us hit that white ball with a four-foot club, connecting at a sweet spot the size of a dime … absolutely amazing! Let's give this body some respect and treat it right so it will be up to this task for many years to come – ***Pain Free.***

CHAPTER 2

FACTORS INFLUENCING YOUR GAME

FACTORS INFLUENCING YOUR GAME

Most golfers share one goal: to get the ball in the cup with the least number of shots without experiencing pain. Sounds simple. But before we set out on the path of eliminating the pain and improving our game, we must first understand that five factors influence our game.

The Five Factors Influencing Your Game
1   **The Course**
2   **Acumen**
3   **Equipment**
4   **Mental Attitude**
5   **Physical Ability**

Let's take a closer look at these factors. The first two, **the course** and **acumen** (our natural ability for golf) cannot be altered; we must take them as they are. The next two factors, **equipment** and **mental attitude,** are changeable and are the primary factors every golfer works on. The fifth and final factor, **physical ability,** is the most neglected area ... and the one that allows for the greatest immediate improvement. For the golfer, physical ability is "the final frontier" on the journey to better golf, and it is the area that we will examine most closely.

In my seminars, I like to use the analogy of a sports-car race to illustrate this material. Let's think of our golf game as such a race, with us as drivers. Each driver entered in the race has the same ultimate aim: to pass the checkered flag first.

1   **The Course** is our racetrack. It's the same for all the drivers. Each course presents its own unique challenges; try as we may, we cannot change its physical layout.

2   **Acumen** can be defined as our natural talent for something. For example, some people are good with numbers or have an ear for music. In sports-car racing, it's that inexplainable "feel" a driver has behind the wheel, the instinct that tells him when to pass another driver on a hairpin curve. Jeff Gordon would be a good example of a driver with tremendous acumen. Similarly, Michael Jordan and Tiger Woods possess great acumen in their respective sports.

Unfortunately, we cannot change the degree of acumen we have – we are born with it.

3 **Equipment,** let's think of Equipment as the car itself. The car is essential to our performance, but the car will not make you a successful driver. In golf, we go to great lengths to change our equipment –our clubs, our shoes, etc. – but we usually see little or no improvement in our game.

4 **Mental Attitude** is the mindset we will have when we're racing. It's the mental toughness that will help us come from behind or rebound after an accident. There are hundreds of books dedicated to improving a golfer's "mental game," but you won't be able to "think" or "will" the ball into the hole – you have to actually hit it there.

5 **Physical Ability** is the final and most important factor that influences your game, and the one that is least explored. Think of physical ability as the actual driver of the racecar. If the driver has physical flaws, he/she will not be able to perform effectively. If you've entered a race and cannot perform the necessary physical tasks, it won't matter what the track looks like, what your mental attitude is or what tires you have on the car, you won't win the race.

As you might have guessed, Physical Ability is another way of describing the body. As we discussed in Chapter One, the body is the most important element behind playing golf successfully and pain free. So often we go for the "quick fix" – changing our equipment or buying a new instructional video – but unless we get our body working effectively, we will never see significant improvement – and never win the race, much less finish it.

As already mentioned, this book focuses on evaluating and improving your physical abilities. Physical ability has four components:

The Four Components of Physical Ability
1   **Flexibility**
2   **Balance**
3   **Endurance**
4   **Strength**

1   **Flexibility** is what you need to go through the long range of motions of an effective, well-balanced golf swing. This is the most important component and the most commonly overlooked.

2   **Balance** is, simply, the ability to stay centered on the ground through-out the golf swing and not to fall over. The importance of balance cannot be stressed enough and I have devoted a chapter to it later in the book.

3   **Endurance** is also an important part of physical ability. It is what enables us to maintain flexibility and balance for the 3–4 hours we spend on the course. We all know habitual golfers who are up every day to tee off at the crack of dawn, but they can hardly walk to the second tee without pain. How can they expect to make it through 18 holes calmly?

4   **Strength** is not that important for golf. Since the club and ball weigh so little, not a lot of actual strength is required for golf. Strength only becomes important once your swing is grooved. If you are struggling with your swing it makes no sense to increase your muscle mass; in fact, it will worsen your swing!!!

We will examine these four components of physical ability in greater detail later in the book. Now I'd like to end this chapter by asking you to grab one of your golf clubs, and then join me for the next step of *Pain-Free Golf, The Perfect Golf Swing.*

CHAPTER 3

THE PERFECT GOLF SWING

THE PERFECT GOLF SWING

There is no golf swing that is perfect for everyone. There are as many different golf swings as there are golfers. The main principle of an effective golf swing is that the club head meets the ball squarely at impact. How we get to this point depends on the individual golfer's body and its restrictions. Each golfer has unique experiences, traumas and injuries that cause particular restrictions within that person's biomechanical system, i.e., the body. These experiences make our golf swing uniquely our own. That is why when a golfer tries to emulate another golfer's swing he or she is unsuccessful.

How many times have we seen a weekend golfer who is 5 ft. 10 inches, 240 pounds and 55 years of age try to copy the golf swing of a professional golfer who is 180 pounds, 6 ft. 3 inches and 35 years old? Or watched a golf teacher prescribe one particular type of swing – the one that works best for him – to all of his students, regardless of their sex, age or weight. That approach is like trying to cram your foot into a shoe four sizes too small – it doesn't fit. It is a formula that spells disaster and frustration.

We have all hit that "perfect shot." But when we try to repeat it with any consistency, we find it next to impossible. The reason the pros are able to do it, day in and day out, is because they have – through predictability and repetition – found their perfect golf swing. What I mean by "predictability" is the ability to consistently reproduce the same motion over and over in different situations – on the fairway, in lies, or in bunkers. **Achieving predictability is essential if you are to develop an effective/efficient golf swing.**

EFFECTIVE AND EFFICIENT

In order for our golf move to be **effective,** we must be able to hit the ball **well;** for our move to be **efficient** we must be able to hit the ball **well with minimal effort.** Only then does it make sense to work on your strength.

Before you improve your performance you must be able to execute the basics:

1   As long as you don't have a consistent swing, work on removing your restrictions by increasing your flexibility.

2   Once you have a more consistent swing, start to also work on your strength.

Pain-Free Golf will educate you about your own body – and its restrictions – so that you can find the golf swing that is perfect for you. Though the golf swing is as personal and individual as our own lives, there are certain basic principles that make a golf swing efficient. Let's look at them:

Basic Principles

Contributing To A Successful Golf Swing

1   **Balance**
2   **Movement**
3   **Sequence**

1   **Balance** You must start in a balanced position. In every movement, balance is the basis for success. It's what enables Kobe Bryant to hit a fall-away jumper at the buzzer, and what allows Mark McGwire to hit one of his towering home runs. If you are off balance, your body will start to compensate and you will never have a smooth, repeatable golf swing.

Balance is the basis for success.

11

2 **Movement** The movement we are striving for is the motion of a pendulum. The pendulum movement starts from the center, then swings left and right, with the axis always staying the same. Remember your grandparents' cuckoo clock? The movement starts from the center as the large parts of the clock's lever need to move first; then the movement is transferred to the rest of the parts in a simple, easy motion. At the end of Chapter 2, I asked you to grab one of your golf clubs. Pick it up now and hold the club between your thumb and index fingers.

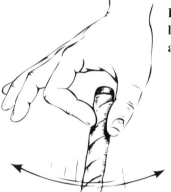

Pendulum motion swings left and right while retaining a consistent axis.

Then, slowly, let the golf club swing to the left and then to the right. Notice how the club stays on the same path as it crosses the center point or "impact point." This pendulum movement is what we want in our golf swing, with the club head hitting the ball at the same place every time.

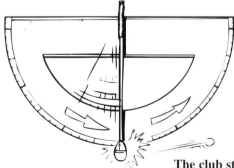

The club stays on the same path as it crosses the "impact point."

3 **Sequence** There is a very definite and specific sequence to the golf
swing. A lot of times this sequence is "off" and is usually referred
to as "swing flaws." With some repetitive training we can train our
brain and muscles to turn on this sequence. Pain, tightness and loss
of balance interfere with this "flow" and we feel "out of synch."
Let's break it down.

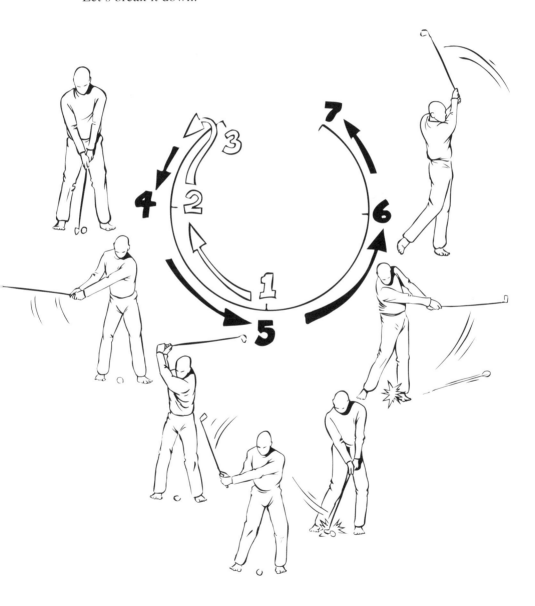

COMPONENTS OF THE GOLF SWING

The following components are extremely important to follow through in sequence. As you can tell by the order of the body movements, certain muscle groups need to "fire" smoothly, one after the other, to allow you to go through these positions efficiently. As you read through the following sequence, pick up your club and try each movement.

1 **Address**

2 **Take-Away**

3 **Top of the Back Swing**

4 **Down Swing**

5 **Impact**

6 **Follow Through**

7 **Finish**

1 **Address** The address is the most important part of the golf swing. This is where we find and set our balance and athletic "power position." Your weight should be divided equally through the heels, the middle, and the balls of the feet. To test your balance, rock forward on the toes, rock back on the heels, and settle into the center. With your feet balanced, bend your knees and hips slightly, arms hanging loosely while holding the club. Your neck should be relaxed; your shoulders should be soft and pulled back slightly, with the stomach muscles slightly engaged.

The Address

COMPONENTS OF THE GOLF SWING

2 **Take-Away** This is the phase where we start to draw the club to the side – just like the pendulum. The trunk and arms move as one piece, and then the weight shift is initiated. This is a natural winding-up motion.

3 **Top Of The Back Swing** This is the position where many problems occur. Many people think they have to have a long backswing to hit the ball far, and, consequently, go beyond a place of balance. The spine should be straight, knees and hips remaining slightly bent, with the trunk rotated over the hips, hips shifted to the side and rotated over the legs. As the wrists move into "tray" position, the neck stays in place. Check your balance.

4 **Down Swing** All movement and weight shift is initiated with the hips and then the arms, hands and club follow.

The Down Swing

5 **Impact** The hips continue to rotate slightly towards the target, with the trunk and shoulders moved behind the hips. The hands and forearms are in neutral position, and the neck stays still.

The Impact

6 **Follow Through** As the hips rotate more towards the target, the knees are still bent. The neck position stays constant as the hands and forearms unwind.

The Follow Through

7 **Finish** As the swing finishes, the weight shift is completed. The hips have rotated completely towards the target, together with the trunk and shoulders; the elbows and wrists are bent, and the neck releases at the end of the follow through.

The Finish

You can see how your body needs to be in a position of balance and power throughout this complicated movement. If your body experiences restrictions, tightness, soreness or pain during any of these stages, it will not let you hit the ball smoothly, effectively or on target. Returning to our racecar analogy – "If there is a problem with the engine, you will never win the race."

MUSCLE SEQUENCING – "THE BICYCLE CHAIN"

All ranges of motions, functions, and movements are basically different muscles switching on and off as they are controlled by the brain to create a sequential movement. I compare this sequential movement to that of a bicycle chain. Each segment or link in the bicycle chain has a particular hookup to the next link. All of these links need to move together in sequence over a sprocket in order to accelerate the bicycle forward. The medical term for this sequence is a "closed kinetic chain." Now, imagine that you have a couple of links within the bicycle chain that are rusted together. Every time that these two links move over the sprocket you hear a little clink and you feel the reverberation throughout the bicycle.

Just like rusty links in a chain, a restricted joint affects how a limb moves throughout its function.

A joint which is restricted in a particular motion has an effect on how that limb moves throughout its whole function. For example, if you have a shoulder problem and you are standing in the address position, your body will already know that if it goes into a full backswing, the shoulder will hurt. As a result, you will develop a compensation motion in your swing, and will not be able to smoothly go through the pendulum movement.

In the next section of the book we will examine our body's machine more closely, concentrating on how our muscles function and why pain develops. Then, understanding how the problems develop, we will start to confront them, by taking the self-evaluation test that follows. The evaluation will lead us to exercises to treat our particular set of restrictions, so we can continue on our course to playing happier, healthier golf.

CHAPTER 4

HOW YOUR BODY WORKS

HOW YOUR BODY WORKS

In order to give you a greater appreciation of what happens when we take the body through the golf swing, I'm going to explain how the body actually works. I promise you, I'll keep it light and easy.

Our body is a phenomenal piece of equipment. Unlike most other structures that are built to stand, the body is narrower at the bottom than at the top; i.e., our shoulders are wider than our feet. The body is truly an architectural wonder. Not only does this structure stand, it walks, jumps, swings a golf club, and so forth.

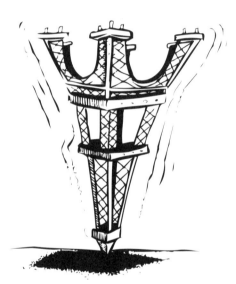

Most structures that stand have a wide bottom base.

Our body structure has a narrower bottom – yet it stands, walks, jumps, swings a golf club and . . .

BONES, MUSCLES, LIGAMENTS, JOINTS . . .

In our body, we have **bones, muscles** and **ligaments.** Ligaments hold bones together; at the point where the bones meet, there are **joints.** The muscles are attached to the bones and move the bones in particular directions.

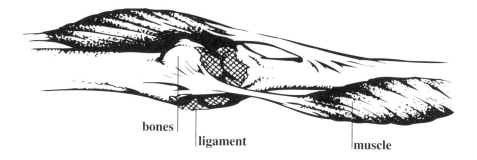

bones | ligament | muscle

If the muscles are tight, the bones won't move or perform effectively. All these movements are guided by **control mechanisms,** signals that go from the brain down to our joints. Then, signals called **feedback mechanisms** are sent from the joints back to the brain. Both mechanisms are processed through the **nerves.**

In order to produce a smooth movement – such as the golf swing – muscles must be controlled in sequence by these mechanisms. Try to pick up a cup of coffee from a table; notice that the arm needs to move forward, the wrist needs to be cocked, the fingers have to open ... all while maintaining our balance. If we have controlled our muscles in sequence, our fingers close around the cup, and we can lift up the cup without spilling the coffee. If you try the same movement in a different sequence, you will surely spill the coffee.

In the last chapter, we talked about the "closed kinetic chain." Here is where that sequential chain really counts. In order for us to pick up that coffee cup – or successfully perform any movement that requires fine motor skills – all the links in the chain must move smoothly. Now you can understand why hitting that little ball at the sweet spot with your club is so challenging!

THE BRAIN: OUR BODY'S COMPUTER

The brain acts as a central computer in this sequence of movements, organizing structures to move in unison and sequence. The feedback mechanisms from our body to our brain serve as controls so that we can stand, lie down, bend forward, etc. They also directly affect our posture and balance.

These feedback mechanisms are only overridden by **pain feedback mechanisms.** If your range of motion brings you to a joint that is sore or a muscle that is hurting, the pain information will override the need for sequential movement and stop your body from moving in that direction. If you have ever sprained an ankle, you know what I mean. It is not easy to put any weight on that ankle and you limp. The brain, subconsciously sensing the area of pain, wants to protect the injured tissues.

Injured Tissues: What Happens and Why

Muscles and ligaments are tissues that need circulation in order to have normal flexibility, pliability and oxygenation. Fresh blood carries oxygen and nutrients; motion and movement bring fresh blood to the tissues. Our bodies respond to a lack of blood supply and lack of oxygenation with a hardening of tissues. When tissues are pliable, flexible and full of nutrients, they hardly ever hurt.

**Healthy tissue is pliable,
flexible and hardly ever hurts.**

Typically, tissues that hurt are hard and rigid and have not moved for a long time. Ligaments become shorter and muscles become tight, decreasing the joint's range of motion and the pliability of the muscle, and therefore decreasing the blood flow even further.

**Unhealthy tissue is hard, rigid
and results in pain.**

To sum it up: Long-standing decreased range of motion and function in an area will cause the hardening of tissues, which results in pain.

Now if we take a hardened, achy joint with a restricted range of motion through the fast-paced, long-range golf swing, we hammer those hardened tissues again and again. The only thing we will accomplish is to cause trauma (and further pain) which will cause swelling in the muscles and, because of the lack of blood supply, the area will not repair well.

PAIN: WHAT WE CAN LEARN FROM IT

In some ways, pain is actually a good thing. Pain lets us know that there is something wrong, and that there are problems that need to be addressed. Let's take a look at how pain correlates to the golf swing.

As mentioned in the previous chapter, the golf swing consists of several motions that need to be followed through in a sequential manner. If any of the movements have a restriction, pain, soreness or aches will be felt in a particular joint. The irritation of a tight tissue being taken through a fast-paced, long-range motion on a repetitive basis (let's say a hundred golf swings in an afternoon) is significant. The physiological event is such that the irritation will make the joint swollen, hot and sore. These are the symptoms of **inflammation.**

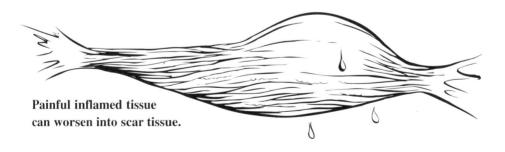

**Painful inflamed tissue
can worsen into scar tissue.**

If the golfer continues to play over a prolonged period of time (days, weeks, or months), the inflammation will then form **scar tissue.** Scar tissue is the body's effort to stabilize and solidify an area that has been repeatedly irritated. If you've ever worn a shoe that is tight, your foot usually gets an irritation. If you continue walking in the shoe, you will get a blister and the area will get inflamed. If you walk in the same shoe over a long period of time – weeks, months – the body will form a callus, or scar tissue, at the point of the inflammation. The same principle holds true for ligaments, bones and muscles.

I hope that now you have a good idea as to why so many golfers are hurting. It should also be very easy to understand why no golf club, no golf ball, no golf shoes, no lucky charm, or no magnet will get you out of this vicious cycle of pain. The only way to address the pain is with the appropriate limbering, flexibility exercise or some other helpful tools to increase the circulation in the hardened area. By increasing the oxygenation in the tissue and lengthening the fibers that have hardened and shortened, we reestablish a more appropriate function for the golf swing. All of a sudden, the need for this type of approach to golf becomes very obvious. In other words, we have found hope amidst the pain.

Pain Care

We can divide pain (including aches and soreness) into two types: **acute pain** and **chronic pain.** Acute pain refers to a sharp, intense pain that has recently been inflicted; chronic pain describes a long-standing, nagging pain. First, let's examine acute pain.

Imagine you are on the golf course, playing well and enjoying the day, when, all of a sudden, you hit a fat shot. The vibration of the shaft reverberates through your arms and gives you significant pain in your forearm, neck and shoulder. What has just happened is that your tissues experienced the shock of going through an excessive range of motion at a very fast pace with an immediate stop, literally damaging some of these tissues apart. Your brain perceives this sensation as an injury, and the first thing that your body wants to do is to curl up and bring that forearm close to your body in order to protect it. As tissues go into spasms, your brain is sending overriding feedback mechanisms to the rest of your body, not letting it function the way it should during the golf swing. At this moment, the chances are very slim that you will finish a good round of golf; it would be best to stop.

To treat a situation like the one just described, I recommend **"R I C E"** thera-py – **R**est, **I**ce, **C**ompression, **E**levation. Any acute injury will be swollen, hurtful, reddened and can benefit from this type of approach. With acute pain we want to decrease the blood supply and get rid of swelling.

An acute muscle injury will be swollen, hurtful and reddened, and needs cooling down.

The other type of pain you might have experienced is chronic pain, that dull achy and persistent nag. With activity, chronic pain is aggravated into a sharper pain and tends to swell up. Chronic pain should be approached with a deep-penetrating heat treatment combined with easy stretching. With chronic pain we want to increase the blood supply and oxygenation going to the hardened tissues to soften them up.

**Chronic pain should be approached
with deep penetrating heat treatment.**

BALANCE & POSTURE: SUPPORT IS EVERYTHING

How do balance and posture fit into all of this? As we saw in our examination of the golf swing, balance and posture are of vital importance in stabilizing your body in the address position. It is quite easy to imagine that if your body is out of balance and you are about to go through a certain range of motion, your brain perceives that your body feels unstable. When a golfer is not balanced at address, and goes through the golf swing with excessive motions, the brain has to work overtime just to keep the golfer on his feet. If the brain is preoccupied with keeping you balanced, it will not be able to control the golf swing with accuracy on a repeated basis. Consistency and predictability go out the window. Remember, all the mechanisms in the body prescribe to the survival needs of our system. If the brain feels that the body is threatened – whether through pain or instability – it will go into its protective mechanism modes and start shutting things down. When you are going through a golf swing and your body senses that you are going to be out of balance, it is not going to be able to concentrate on squaring the club head at the moment of impact.

This is why being **balanced at address** is of extreme importance. Proper balance and posture will let your brain more accurately sense the feedback mechanisms during the complicated process of your golf swing.

The following diagram illustrates what I refer to as the **power position.** The power position gives the golfer maximum support and balance at the address stage. Notice that the extremities are close to the gravity line. If you watch sports like karate, boxing and baseball, you'll also see that impact occurs when the extremities are close to the body center. The closer you are to your power position, the less energy you spend on maintaining balance. This allows you to be more effective in your motion, and to hit the ball better with fewer injuries.

Pick up your club and set your body in the power position. Feels good, doesn't it? Now go into the forward reach with your weight on your toes and swing the club . Then repeat the same movement with your weight on your heels. Notice the difference: When your body was in the power position it felt centered; when you put all your weight on your toes or your heels you felt off-balance.

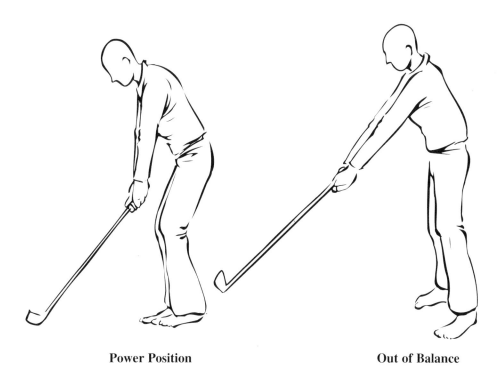

Power Position   **Out of Balance**

THE GOLF "MOVE"

Let's look at the actual "golf move" involved in your swing.

Golf demands a very unique type of movement. Most sports happen on one or two planes of action. In golf, our body actually needs to perform motions in <u>three</u> different planes:

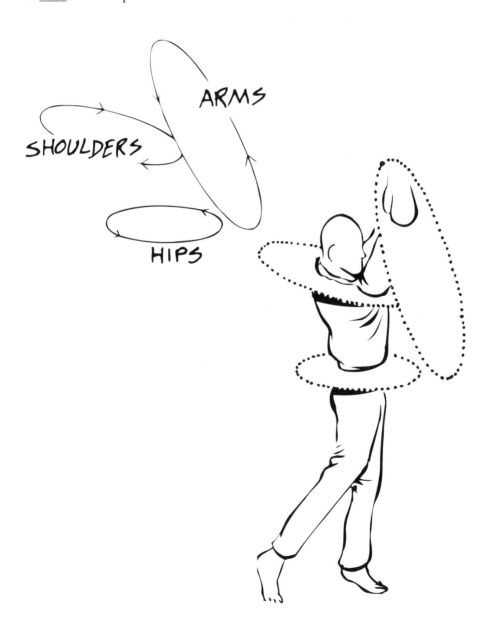

1 **The hips** move on a rotational plane and are at a slight angle to the floor.

2 **The shoulders and trunk** move into a rotational movement at a steeper angle to the floor.

3 **The arms** move the club head in an almost vertical plane to the floor.

Our brain needs to correlate all the muscles, bones, and ligaments moving in these three different planes. And it must make sure that the movements do the following: **a)** occur at the same time, **b)** are accurate, **c)** can be made on a repeated basis, **d)** occur at a very high speed. All these different elements and concerns comprise what I call the **Golf Move.** It is one of the hardest movements of any sport, and the reason why the game of golf is so difficult. The neurological control and feedback mechanisms are extremely complex. If your brain and body sense pain and/or injury, you can imagine how many nerve fibers, muscle fibers, ligaments, etc. need to correlate in this compensation. If you have a problem in any of these motions, you will have a problem with your swing.

SUMMARY

To recap what we have discussed so far:

1 **The Golf Swing**

An efficient golf swing has an easy flow and uses little effort.

2 **Your Brain**

Your brain tells your body how to move.

3 **Your Body**

Your body tells your brain what has happened and whether you are able to complete the movements without pain (or what you need to do to avoid the pain).

4 **Proper Balance, Posture and Flexibility are Essential**

In order for your brain and body to coordinate the difficult move of the golf swing, you must maintain proper balance, posture and flexibility.

5 **Three Planes of Body Movement**

The golf move is a unique process that requires the body to make movements in 3 different planes. If there is a problem in any plane, the swing will not be effective or efficient.

6 **Pain Can Indicate Treatment Measures**

You can use pain as an indicator of what is wrong in your golf swing and can take measures to treat it accordingly.

Now that we understand how the body works and why we experience pain and lack of control in the golf swing, let's go to the next step of the process: *the self-evaluation test.*

CHAPTER 5

GOLF FITNESS EVALUATION

HOW TO TAKE THE SELF-EVALUATION TEST

PREPARING FOR THE TEST

In this chapter we are going to discuss how to prepare for and take the self-evaluation test. Before we begin, please ask yourself the following questions:

1 Have you been experiencing your pain for a very long period of time?

2 Does the pain feel sharp and debilitating?

3 Have you been experiencing numbness and tingling in any of the extremities?

4 Have you been trying to heal the pain for quite some time without any results?

If you can answer "yes" to any of these questions, do yourself a favor: Visit your chiropractic/medical doctor, physical therapist, or anyone in the medical field who is experienced in the treatment of sports injuries and rehabilitation and get some treatment.

This book is in no way geared towards self-diagnosing your pain/injury, nor is it going to be the "fix" for disorders or diseases. Use the book as a guide for clarity about your condition, and then go treat it accordingly.

The next word of advice that I want to give you is to **be honest** with yourself during this test. You can do the test by yourself in front of a mirror or, even better, do it together with a friend or fellow golfer who has the integrity to give you an accurate reading. For comfort and ease, it is best to do each evaluation in a pair of shorts and tank top. Before you actually do each test, read through it and go through the motions to see whether or not you understand how these motions are supposed to be done. Don't go into your pain. **Honor your limits.** Go slow and don't be in a hurry; these 20 minutes will make a change for a lifetime of better, more enjoyable golf.

COMPONENTS OF THE GOLF SWING

HOW TO RATE YOURSELF

For all the movements we are testing, the range of motion has been broken into four areas. The rating system goes from **1** to **4:**

1 If you are experiencing **pain** in a motion, you will rate yourself with a **1.**

2 If you are experiencing **restriction** in a motion, you will rate yourself a **2.**

3 If you are going through a **full range of motion without pain,** you will rate yourself a **3.**

4 If you are going through an **extra-long range of motion without pain,** you will rate yourself a **4.**

HOW TO FOLLOW THE GRAPHICS FOR THE 1-4 ZONES

The description of each motion is accompanied by a graphic. In this graphic, we have broken down the movement into four quadrants. After noting your range of motion for a particular movement, look at the illustration and locate the quadrant where your motion stops and record your score. When you perform the movement, you should stop at the spot where the pain just barely starts or where your restriction of movement begins. Remember that the brain and the feedback mechanisms already control and start a compensation pattern at the beginning of restriction. So going **into** the painful area is not an accurate reading as it relates to this test. You have to stop short of the pain so that your body does not engage its compensatory mechanisms. Remember, this evaluation process is not about "good" or "bad," flunking or passing. This test is about figuring out your body's own restrictions and how to overcome them. It is not a test of your **potential** but of where your **limits** currently are. Part of what we need to overcome is our inherent wish to perform well or to out-perform someone else.

HOW TO ADD UP YOUR SCORE

Record Your Score as You Go After performing each movement, record your score. It is very important to record your results as you go along because, if you wait until the end, chances are you won't remember your scores.

Tally the Scores to Identify Your Rating When you have completed the final movement, tally your scores under the columns for each numerical rating. First, add up the number of **1** ratings you've earned, then the number of **2** ratings, then the number of **3** & **4** ratings. Then, subtotal these amounts at the bottom of the page. Finally, add up your subtotaled scores to reach your final rating.

HOW TO LOCATE YOUR PROBLEM AREAS

I have broken down the golf swing into 21 different components – by body part. If a golfer experiences difficulty in any one of these 21 components during the evaluation, then he/she is going to experience difficulties during the golf swing in that body part. The test lets you know your body's areas of restriction; the next step is to do the exercises I have designed to address those particular areas of restriction. For example: If you experience restrictions in three of the shoulder-area movements, go to the section of shoulder exercises and do those.

MOVEMENTS FOR GOLF FITNESS EVALUATION

NECK

1　Rotation
2　Side Bend

SHOULDERS

3　Abduction to the Top
4　Forward Crossovers
5　Shoulder Adduction
6　Internal Rotation
7　External Rotation

UPPER BACK

8　Flex
9　Extension

ARMS & WRIST

10　Pronation
11　Supination
12　Adduction
13　Abduction

TRUNK

14　Standing Lateral Flex
15　Lying Twist
16　Seated Rotation

LOWER BACK
& HAMSTRINGS

17　Standing Lateral Flex

CALVES

18　Seated Forward Bend with Toe Pull

HIP FLEXIBILITY
& BALANCE

19　Standing Weight Shift
20　Balance Test

FOREARMS

21　Forearm Strength Test

NECK

1 ROTATION

Turn your head to the right side as far as you can without pain. Then turn it to the left side.

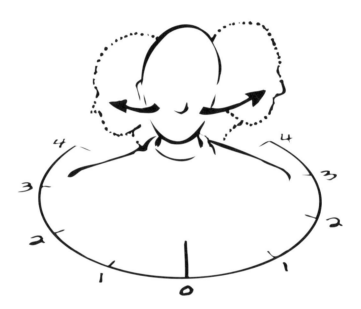

Circle Your Score and Add to Tally Totals on Page 61

SCORE   1   2   3   4   _____

2 SIDE BEND

Tilt your neck to the right side without moving your shoulders.
Then tilt your neck to the left side.

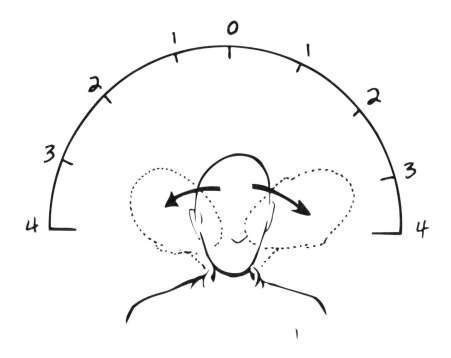

Circle Your Score and Add to Tally Totals on Page 61

SCORE   1   2   3   4   _____

SHOULDERS

3 ABDUCTION TO THE TOP

With your arms at your sides, turn the palms of your hands outward.

Then raise your arms above your head and bring your palms together, elbows straight, arms in line with your ears.

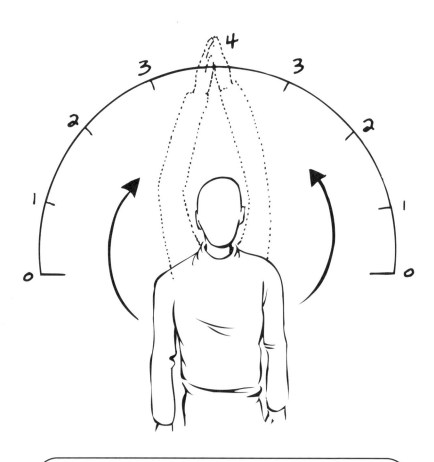

Circle Your Score and Add to Tally Totals on Page 61

SCORE   1   2   3   4   _____

4 FORWARD CROSSOVERS

Raise your arms to shoulder level, keeping both elbows straight.

Bring your right arm across the top of the left arm;
return to the original position.

Now try bringing the left arm across the top of the right arm.

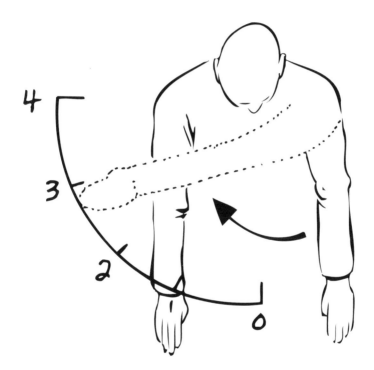

Circle Your Score and Add to Tally Totals on Page 61

SCORE   1   2   3   4   _____

5   SHOULDER ADDUCTION

Put the palms of your hands together and take your hands up to your forehead.

Then try to bring your elbows together.

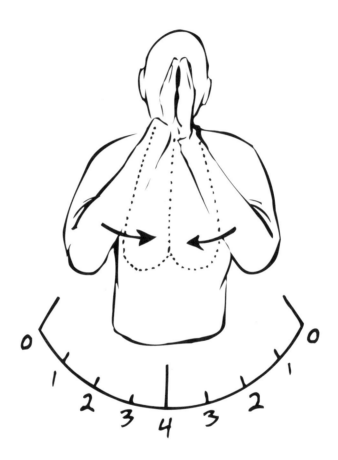

Circle Your Score and Add to Tally Totals on Page 61

SCORE   1   2   3   4   _____

6 INTERNAL ROTATION

Stand with your left arm hanging by its side and your right arm bent in front of you.

Keeping your elbow tucked by your side, open your right forearm out to your side.

Do the other side.

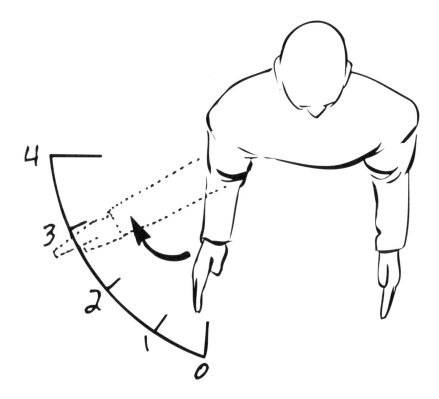

Circle Your Score and Add to Tally Totals on Page 61

SCORE 1 2 3 4 _____

7 EXTERNAL ROTATION

Stand with your left arm hanging by its side and your right arm bent in front of you.

Keeping your elbow tucked by your side, bring your right forearm across your chest.

Do the other side.

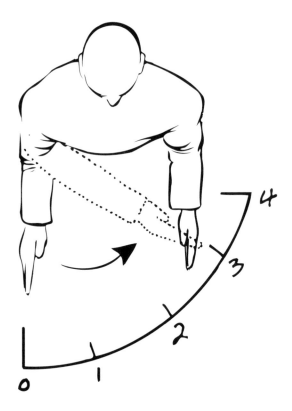

Circle Your Score and Add to Tally Totals on Page 61

SCORE   1   2   3   4   _____

UPPER BACK

8 FLEX

Drop your head slowly to your chest, carefully observing any
pain or restriction.

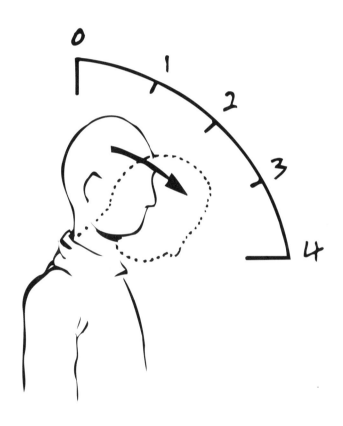

Circle Your Score and Add to Tally Totals on Page 61

SCORE   1   2   3   4   _____

9 EXTENSION

Tilt your head back slowly, as far as you can without pain.
Take extra care to guide the head back – **don't jerk or snap it.**

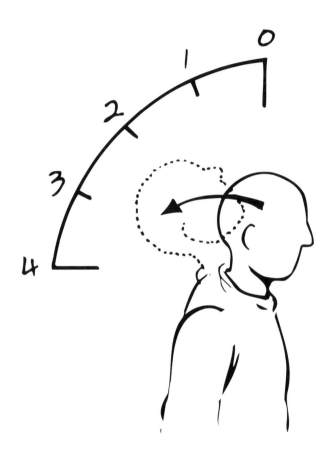

Circle Your Score and Add to Tally Totals on Page 61

SCORE   1   2   3   4   _____

ARMS | WRIST

10 PRONATION

Standing with palms facing up, turn the palms down.

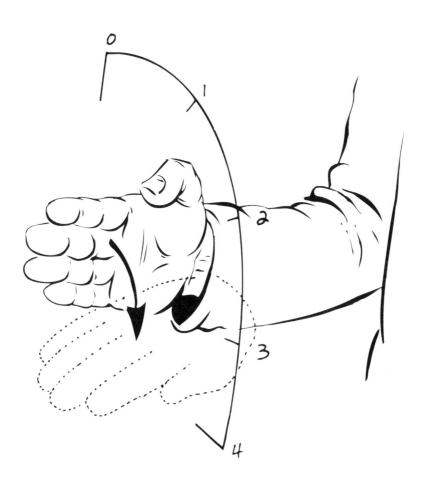

Circle Your Score and Add to Tally Totals on Page 61

SCORE   1   2   3   4   _____

ARMS | WRIST CONTINUED

11 SUPINATION

Standing with palms facing down, turn the palms up.

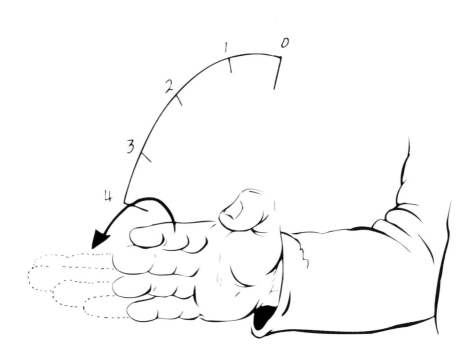

Circle Your Score and Add to Tally Totals on Page 61

SCORE   1   2   3   4   _____

12 ADDUCTION

With palms up, move your wrists inward.

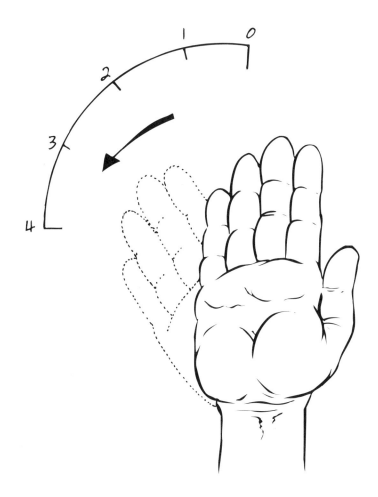

Circle Your Score and Add to Tally Totals on Page 61

SCORE   1   2   3   4   _____

13 ABDUCTION

With raised palms, move your wrists outward.

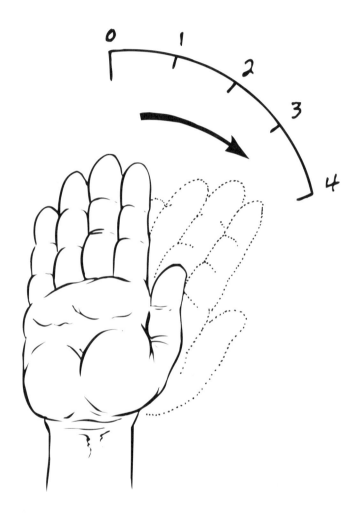

Circle Your Score and Add to Tally Totals on Page 61

SCORE   1   2   3   4   _____

TRUNK

14 STANDING LATERAL FLEX

Keeping your lower body straight, tilt your upper body to the left side by sliding your left hand along the thigh. Do not tilt your head.

Repeat the same movement on the other side.

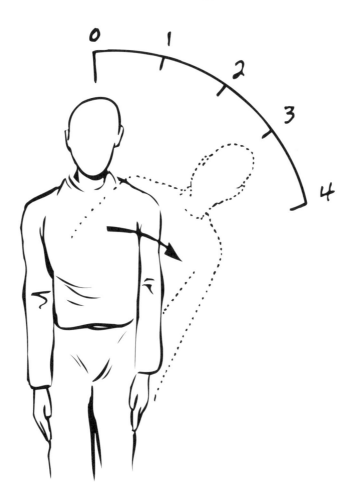

Circle Your Score and Add to Tally Totals on Page 61

SCORE　1　　2　　3　　4　　_____

12 LYING TWIST

Lie on your back with your knees bent, your feet together and both arms stretched out to the sides.

Drop both knees over to the left; then, drop them over to the right. Remember to keep your trunk flat during these movements.

Repeat the same movement on the other side.

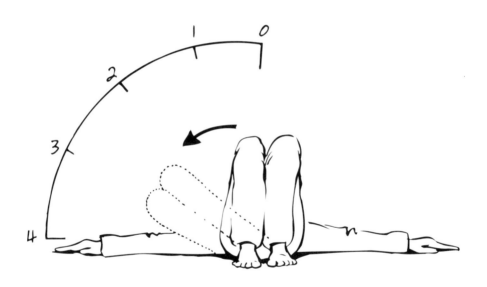

Circle Your Score and Add to Tally Totals on Page 61

SCORE　　1　　　2　　　3　　　4　　———————

13 SEATED ROTATION

Sit with your legs straight out in front of you. Drop both arms in front of your chest and turn the upper body to the right side; return to center and turn your upper body to the left side.

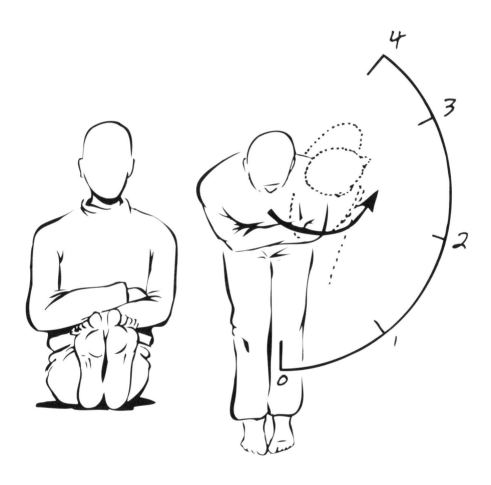

Circle Your Score and Add to Tally Totals on Page 61

SCORE 1 2 3 4 _____

LOWER BACK | HAMSTRING

17 SEATED FORWARD BEND

Sit with your legs straight.

With your arms stretched in front of you, flatten your lower back and gently lean towards your toes .

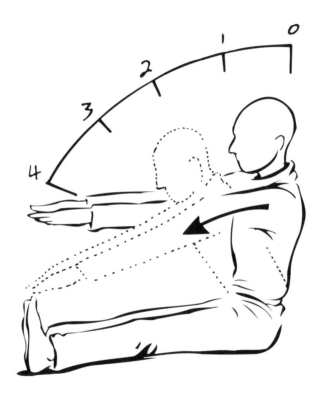

Circle Your Score and Add to Tally Totals on Page 61

SCORE   1   2   3   4   _____

CALVES

18 SEATED FORWARD BEND WITH TOE PULL

Stay in the position described for Seated Forward Bend #17.

This time, pull the toes towards you and lean forward.

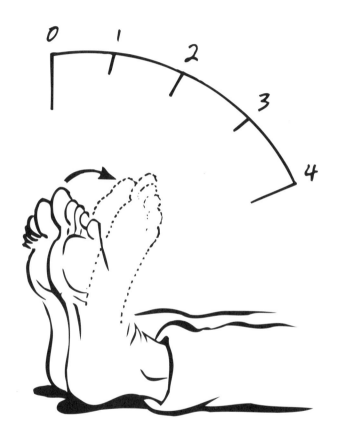

Circle Your Score and Add to Tally Totals on Page 61

SCORE   1   2   3   4   _____

HIP FLEXIBILITY

19 STANDING WEIGHT SHIFT

With your feet set a foot apart, put weight on the left leg and shift the left hip to the side.

Return to center.

Now do the same movement on the right side. Don't lean with your whole body – we just want to isolate and test the outer hip.

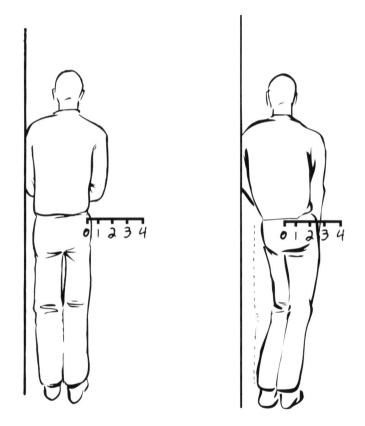

Circle Your Score and Add to Tally Totals on Page 61

SCORE   1   2   3   4   _____

BALANCE

20 BALANCE TEST

Close both eyes and stand on one leg. Measure your ability to balance by counting the amount of time you can keep this position without falling. Counting should begin the moment you close your eyes.

Count up to 5   = **Score 1**
Count 5 to 10   = **Score 2**
Count 11 to 20 = **Score 3**
Count 21 to 30 = **Score 4**

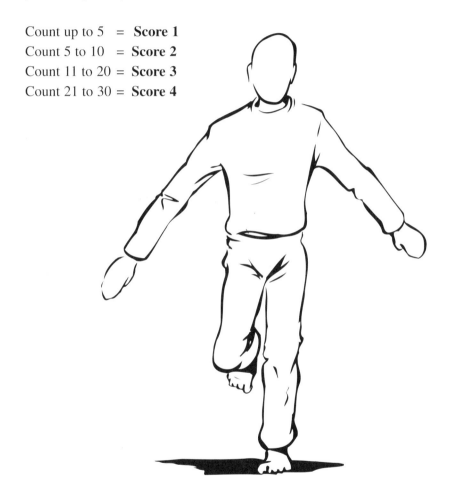

Circle Your Score and Add to Tally Totals on Page 61

SCORE   1   2   3   4   _____

FOREARMS

21 FOREARM STRENGTH TEST

Take a golf club in one hand and let both arms hang at the sides. **Without bending the elbow,** raise the club up to belt level.

Do this movement 5 times   = **Score 1**
Do this movement 10 times = **Score 2**
Do this movement 15 times = **Score 3**
Do this movement 20 times = **Score 4**

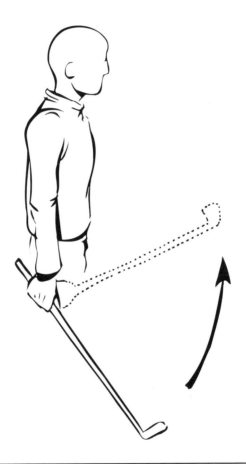

Circle Your Score and Add to Tally Totals on Page 61

SCORE   **1**   **2**   **3**   **4**   _____

GOLF FITNESS EVALUATION SCORECARD

Today's Date _____

I suggest using a #2 pencil. You can reutilize this evaluation
scorecard for ongoing golf fitness self evaluations.

Tally the Score Ratings to Identify Your General Golf Fitness Level

Number of **1** scored	**x1** =	
Number of **2** scored	**x2** =	
Number of **3** scored	**x3** =	
Number of **4** scored	**x4** =	
Your General Golf Fitness Level _____	**total**	

Your Problem Area

Look back at the top of the pages 40-60 indicating the body parts. The area
where you have accumulated the most **1** and **2** scores is the main problem
area **interfering with your golf swing.**

Now proceed to <u>Chapter 6: Golf Fitness Stretches</u>. After reading the introduc-
tion, recall your problematic body area and concentrate your efforts on the
Chapter 6 stretches related to that region. <u>Chapter 8: Golf Fitness Drills</u> out-
lines general limbering drills for the rest of your body.

If I would instruct you to do all the stretches in Chapter 6, chances are you
wouldn't do them. **Focus on removing the restrictions in your problem area
only,** supporting that with general limbering drills in <u>Chapter 8: Golf Fitness
Drills</u> and therapy ball exercises <u>Chapter 7: Golf Fitness Exercises with
Therapy Ball.</u> This limits your time commitment and makes you more likely
to prepare to – *Play Golf Pain Free!*

CHAPTER 6

GOLF FITNESS STRETCHES

STRETCHES

Before you start the stretching exercises, I can't over-emphasize the importance of warming up before stretching. Warming up will increase the blood flow to the muscle, which will speed up the metabolic rate, increase oxygen and nutrients. A healthier tissue is the result.

WARM UP ROUTINE

1 **Start your stretching with 5- to 10-minute fast-walking, swinging the arms at the same time.**

   and/ or

2 **Sit on a Swiss Ball, bounce gently for five minutes.**

You will be surprised at the payoff and how long five minutes are. As a result, your stretching will be much easier, more efficient and effective.

Stretches are supposed to **loosen** tissues **not tear** them. So go easy. Pain is always an indicator of too much!

Some of the movements I want you to **hold;** some of them I want you to **repeat** – so read the instructions! Do both sides where applicable.

Let's start you out with holding the movement for 5 breaths or repeating it for 5 repetitions. Then, over time (days or weeks, depending on how tight you are when you start this process) increase the number of breaths or repetitions to your improved ability.

Now, Go and Enjoy!

OVERVIEW OF STRETCHES FOR BODY AREAS

GENERAL STRETCHES

1 Cobra
2 Low Back Turn
3 X-Factor Stretch
4 Forward Bend
5 Forward Bend w/Golf Club
6 Hock Squat
7 Chest Stretch
8 Side Stretch

FOREARM

1 Door Frame–Forearm
2 Wrist Extensor Stretch
3 Wrist Flexor Stretch

NECK

1 Neck Extension
2 Lateral Bend
3 Forward Lateral Bend
4 Neck Rotations

ARMS | SHOULDERS

1 Upper Arm Rotations
2 Shoulder Stretch
3 Seated Rotator Stretch
4 Rotator Cuff Strength
5 Standing Shoulder Stretch
6 One-Sided Chest Stretch

BACK | HIPS | LEGS

1 Forward Bend w/Golf Club
2 Hamstrings
3 Quadriceps
4 Inside Thighs
5 Outside Hips
6 Seated Hip Stretch
7 Lying Hip Stretch
8 Low Back Turn
9 X-Factor Stretch
10 Chest Stretch

ANKLE

1 Front of Ankle
2 Calf #1
3 Calf #2
4 Calf #3

GENERAL STRETCHES

COBRA STRETCH

Lie on your stomach, put your elbows under your shoulders, keep your pelvis on the floor and gently push up. Keep your buttocks relaxed.

Breathe 5X

NOTES

LOW BACK TURN STRETCH

Lie on back, bend one knee, pull it across to the opposite side
using your hands.

Breathe 5X

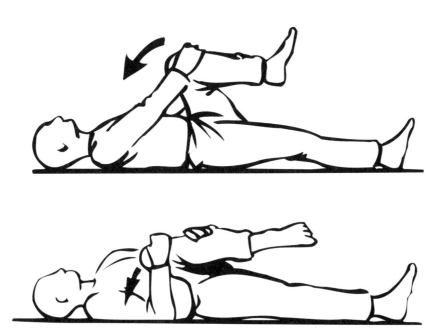

NOTES

X-FACTOR STRETCH

Sitting, bend forward, bring elbow to outside of opposite knee, put other hand on chair or low back, turn your upper body keeping both buttocks down, look toward ceiling.

Breathe 5X

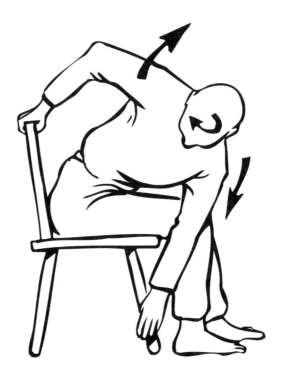

NOTES

FORWARD BEND STRETCH

Slowly bend forward, knees bent, let arms, shoulders and head release, slowly, gently straighten your knees as you breathe.

Breathe 5X

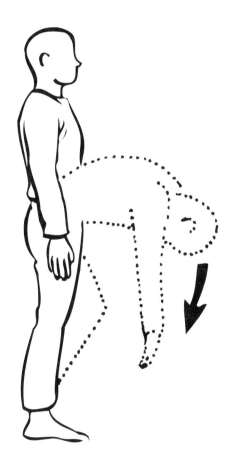

NOTES

FORWARD BEND WITH CLUB STRETCH

Slowly bend forward, knees bent, let arms, shoulders and head release,
slowly, gently straighten your knees as you breathe.

Breathe 5X

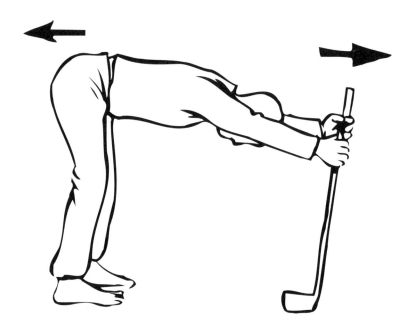

NOTES

HOCK SQUAT

Hold hands on top of golf club, slowly go down into a squat, come off your heels if necessary. Push hands away, keeping your club on the floor.

Breathe 5X

(Push yourself up with the help of a club.)

NOTES

_____

_____

_____

_____

CHEST STRETCH

Stand in doorframe, reach hands out to doorframe, shoulder height, and push chest and body forward without arching your back.

Breathe 5X

NOTES

SIDE STRETCH

Stand next to doorframe, reach one arm across over your head, hold onto doorframe and push your hips into the opposite direction.

Breathe 5X

NOTES

PROBLEM AREA: FOREARM

DOORFRAME STRETCH

Put the back of your hand on the doorframe while keeping your elbow straight, gently push into doorframe and turn your shoulder forward.

Breathe 5X

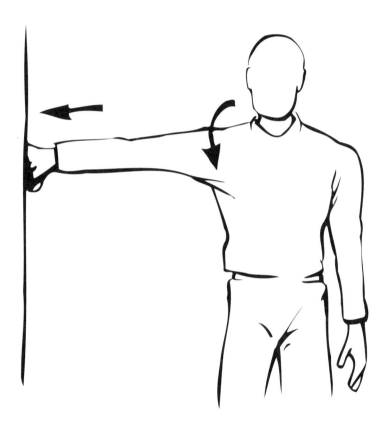

NOTES

WRIST EXTENSOR STRETCH

Palm down; keep your arm level and your elbow straight.

Pull the hand and fingers towards floor and then towards body.

Breathe 5X

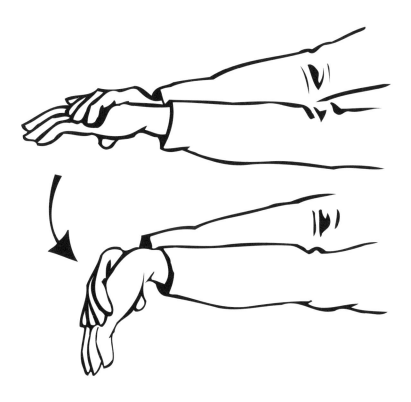

NOTES

_____

_____

_____

_____

_____

WRIST FLEXOR STRETCH

Palm up, elbow straight and arm level, pull your hand and fingers towards the body.

Breathe 5X

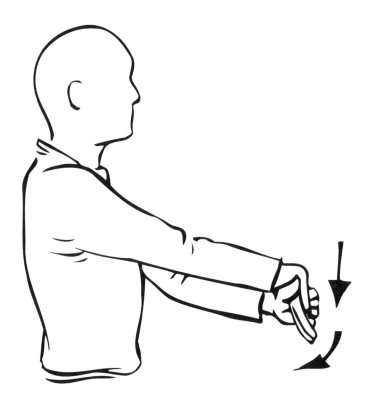

NOTES

PROBLEM AREA: NECK

NECK EXTENSION STRETCH

Put your hands on the back of the neck, fingers interlaced, push your elbows and head backwards, squeezing your shoulder blades together.

Breathe in, release as you breathe out.

Repeat 5X

NOTES

LATERAL BEND

Sitting or standing, hold on with one hand and tilt head to opposite side.

Breathe 5X

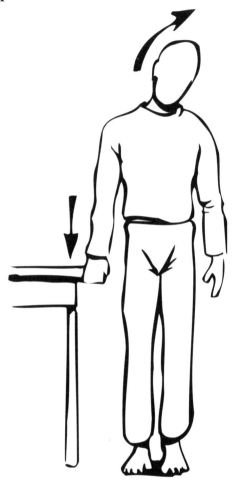

NOTES

FORWARD LATERAL BEND

Sit or stand, hold on with one hand, reach across the top of the head with the other hand and gently turn head halfway, pull forward at an angle, chin towards shoulder.

Breathe 5X

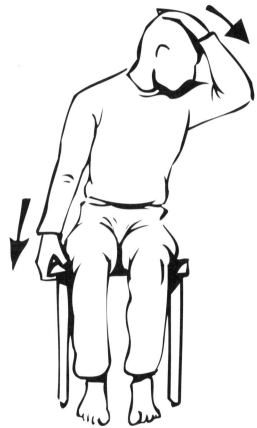

NOTES

NECK ROTATIONS

Sit or stand, turn head to one side leading with your chin.
At the end range, gently push a touch more, breathe, and turn to other side.

Repeat 5X

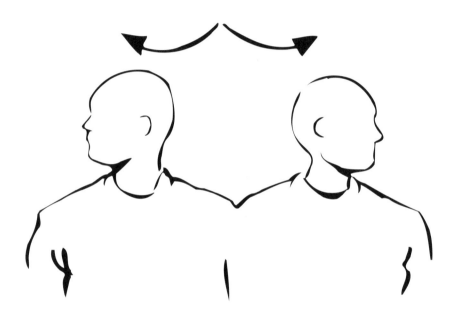

NOTES

_____

_____

_____

_____

_____

PROBLEM AREA: ARMS | SHOULDERS

UPPER ARM ROTATIONS

Lie on back, knees bent, arms straight out to the side. Bend elbow, hands in the air. Gently bring the back of the hands towards the floor. Rest like this.

Breathe 10X

NOTES

SHOULDER STRETCH

Lie on your back, clasp hands, reach up towards the ceiling, and then bring clasped hands gently above the head towards the floor. Hold position.

Breathe 5X

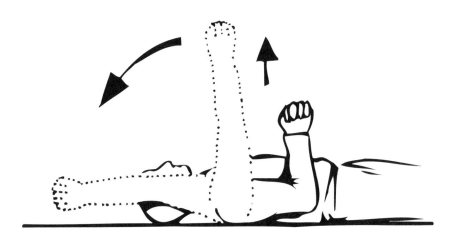

NOTES

SEATED ROTATOR STRETCH

Sitting, cross elbows over and pass opposite knees. Bend forward.

Breathe 5X

NOTES

ROTATOR CUFF STRETCH

Put hand on opposite shoulder, elbow shoulder level, push elbow towards back, letting your hand slide past your shoulder.

Breathe 5X

NOTES

STANDING SHOULDER STRETCH

Stand with your back to the wall, put your hands on the forehead and elbows together. Breathe in as you raise the arms, as much as you can, with your elbows together. Then go up and reach as far as you can, letting your elbows release. Breathe out as you come down to the side with your elbows first, then release forearms and hands, stand with back of the hands to the wall while breathing out completely.

Repeat 5X

NOTES

ONE-SIDED STRETCH

Stand in doorway, reach with one arm, and stretch the chest and that side of body forward.

Breathe 5X

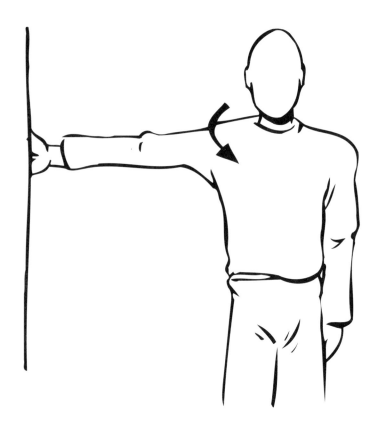

NOTES

_____

_____

_____

_____

_____

PROBLEM AREA: BACK | HIPS | LEGS

FORWARD BEND WITH GOLF CLUB STRETCH

Put your hands on top of golf club; slowly walk backwards until you bend forward. If necessary, keep your knees slightly bent. Breathe. Push your hands from your body while pushing your buttocks back.

Breathe 5X

NOTES

HAMSTRING STRETCH

Put one foot on a chair, keep hips parallel to chair.
Bend standing leg slightly; slowly bend forward with flat back.

Breathe 5X

NOTES

QUADRICEPS STRETCH

Hold on to back of chair, pull foot backwards with the same side hand, keep the knees close to each other and gently pull backwards.

Caution: **Do not arch your back.**

Breathe 5X

NOTES

_____

_____

_____

_____

_____

INSIDE THIGH STRETCH

Standing with legs apart, weight on both feet, shift the hip to one side.

Breathe 5X

NOTES

OUTSIDE HIP STRETCH

Stand close to wall, cross feet, push the hip towards the wall.

Breathe 5X

NOTES

SEATED HIP STRETCH

Sitting, bend and cross one leg, keep the other leg straight. Bring the opposite elbow to bent knee, reach other hand behind you on the floor, and gently turn your body towards the bent knee.

Breathe 5X

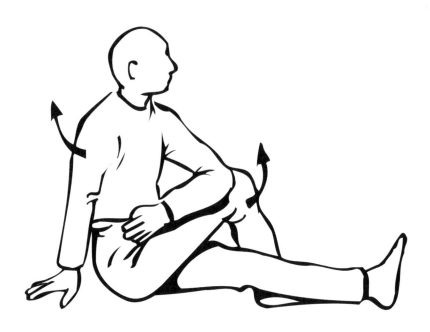

NOTES

LYING HIP STRETCH

Lie on back, arms out, and bend both knees. Bring one ankle to outside of other knee and pull towards the side of top leg.

Breathe 5X

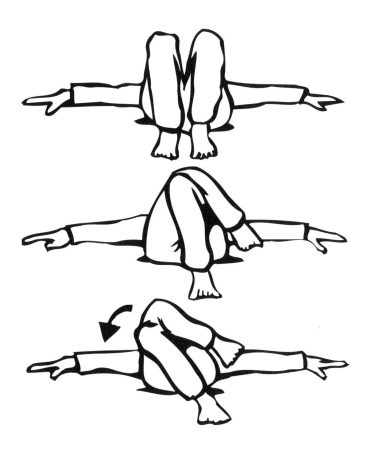

NOTES

LOW BACK TURN STRETCH

Lie on back, bend one knee, pull it across to the opposite side using your hands.

Breathe 5X

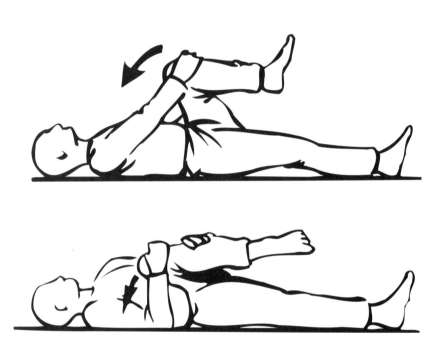

NOTES

_____

_____

_____

_____

X-FACTOR STRETCH

Sitting, bend forward, bring elbow to outside of opposite knee, put other hand on chair or low back, turn your upper body keeping both buttocks down, look towards ceiling.

Breathe 5X

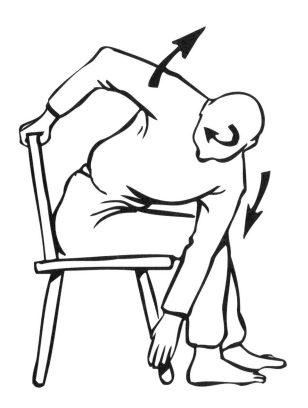

NOTES

CHEST STRETCH

Stand in doorframe, reach hands out to doorframe, shoulder height, and push chest and body forward without arching your back.

Breathe 5X

NOTES

PROBLEM AREA: ANKLES

FRONT ANKLE STRETCH

Sitting, bring one foot under chair, top of foot facing floor.
Gently push ankle towards floor.

Breathe 5X

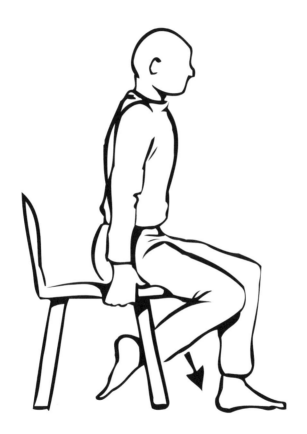

NOTES

CALF STRETCH #1

Face wall, bring one foot back, try to push heel towards floor with straight knee.

Breathe 5X

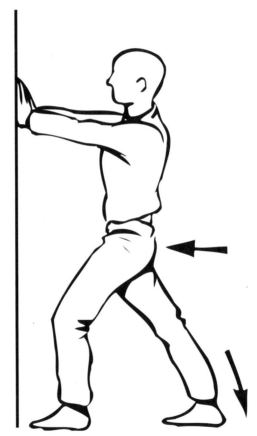

NOTES

CALF STRETCH #2

Face wall, bring one foot back, try to push heel towards floor with knee bent.

Breathe 5X

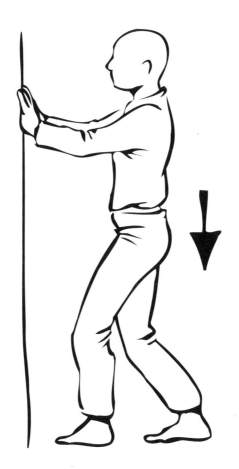

NOTES

_____

_____

_____

_____

_____

CALF STRETCH #3

Stand with balls of feet on step. Let the heels gently draw downwards.

Breathe 5X

NOTES

CHAPTER 7

GOLF FITNESS EXERCISES WITH THERAPY BALL

THERAPY BALL EXERCISES

How to use the therapy ball?

Doing the golf fitness exercises with a therapy ball is actually a lot of fun. Remember how much fun we had as kids playing and rolling around? It is time to revisit these days. The movements that I put together not only work on your golf-specific muscles but also on your sense of balance.

If in the beginning you should feel very unstable on the ball, you can even start out resting the ball against a wall. Otherwise, begin your program with your feet and hands about 4 to 5 feet apart and as you feel more stable bring them closer together.

Otherwise, the same guidelines for stretching apply to the therapy ball: Start slow and easy. Never rush through the exercises. Breathe in as you do contractions, breathe out when you relax. While you are holding exercises, breathe calmly and don't hold your breath. Again, do both sides where applicable.

Challenge yourself, but don't hurt yourself.

Now, Go and Have Fun!

BALL BOUNCE

Sit on ball, feet relaxed on floor, neck and shoulders relaxed;
gently bounce up and down without losing contact with the ball.

Do for 1-2 minutes.

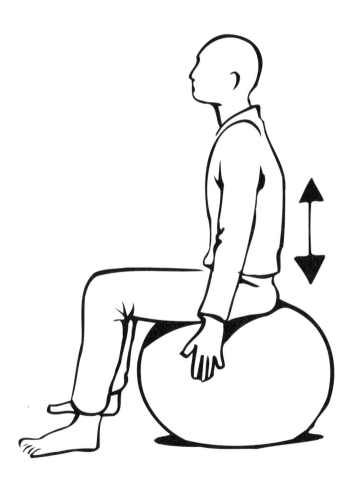

SWING ARM AND BOUNCE

Establish Ball Bounce motion and add swinging the arms, one forward, one back.

Do for 1-2 minutes.

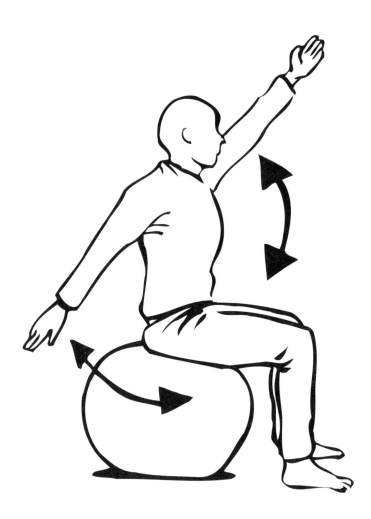

PELVIC TILT

Sit on ball, relaxed, feet on floor, neck and shoulders relaxed.
Roll forward on ball, pulling your buttocks under,
and then roll back on ball while arching your back.

Do for one minute.

PELVIC SIDE TILT

Sit on ball, relaxed, feet on floor, neck and shoulders relaxed.
Roll sideways on ball, tipping buttock down on that side.
Roll sideways to other side.

Do for 1-2 minutes.

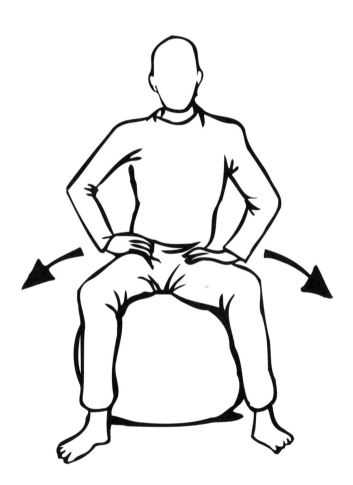

BACK STRETCH

Sit on ball relaxed.

Walk your feet forward while rolling your back onto the ball.

Lean backward and keep the knees bent.

Relax your head and bring your arms out to the side.

Caution: To come out of this position, bring your arms in first.

Rest one minute.

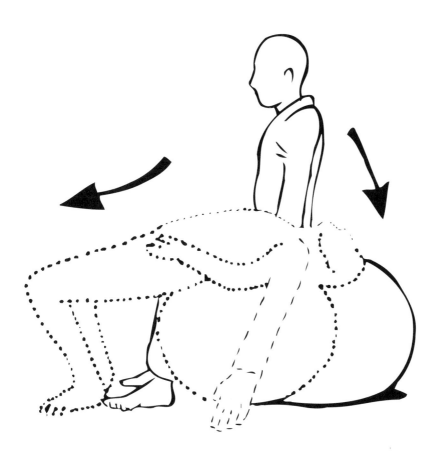

SIT UPS

Start from position indicated for Back Stretch, then cross your arms in front of your chest, lift your head and upper back off the ball. Slowly let go.

Caution: Do not arch your back.

Repeat 10X

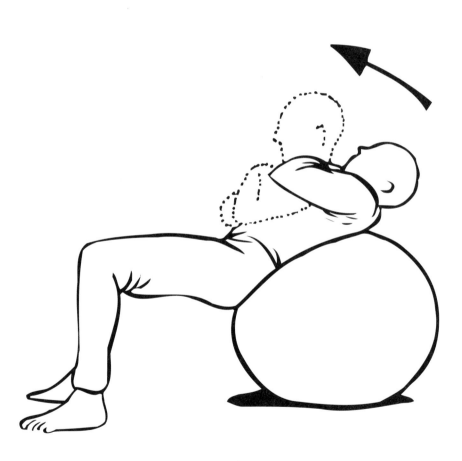

THERAPY BALL EXERCISES CONTINUED

KNEELING SIDE STRETCH

Kneel in front of ball. Rest the hands on top of ball.

Roll ball to one side, keeping knees and buttocks in place.

Hold for 30 seconds and switch sides.

Repeat 5X

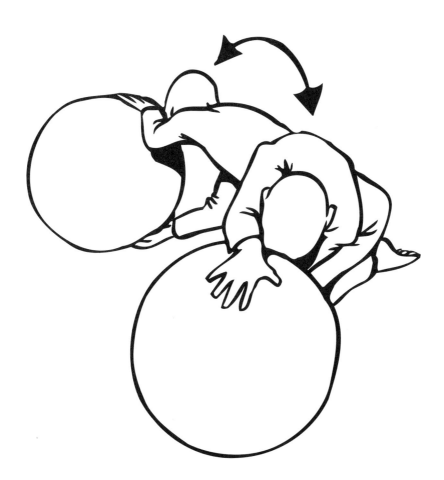

NECK EXTENSION

Rest with stomach on ball, knees on floor, and wrap hands around ball; then, lift head back and release.

Repeat 10X

BACK EXTENSION

Rest with stomach on ball, knees off floor.

Put hands at back of neck with fingers interlaced.

Breathe in, then raise elbows first, then head, then upper body.

Breathe out and release.

Repeat 10X

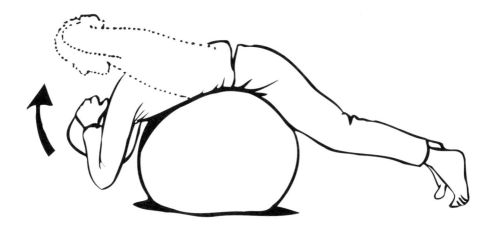

SUPERMAN

Rest with stomach on ball, knees off floor, feet apart.
Raise both outstretched arms up, looking at hands.
Breathe in as you come up.

Repeat 10X

CROSS EXTENSION

Rest with stomach on ball, knees off floor, hands on floor.
Bring one outstretched arm and opposite leg up at same time as you breathe
in. Breathe out and release and do opposite side.

(You can also hold this position for 10 breaths.)

Repeat 10X

TRUNK ROTATION

Rest with stomach on ball, knees on floor.

Lift one hand to side and back towards the ceiling by turning your trunk. Keep both knees on the floor.

Breathe in as you come up.

Breathe out and release, and do opposite side.

(You can also hold this position for 10 breaths.)

Repeat 10X

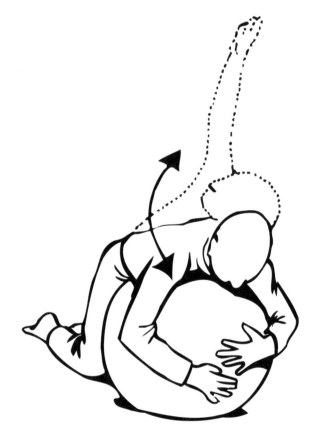

LEG LIFT

Rest with upper and mid back on ball, hands on hips, until your low back is flat (neutral spine).

Hold it here, breathe in, then lift one leg with the knee slightly bent, breathe out and release.

(You can also hold this position for 10 breaths.)

Repeat 10X

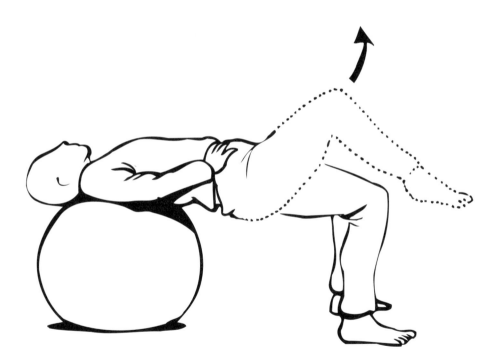

ARM LIFT

Rest with upper and mid back on ball.

Lift buttocks until low back flat (neutral spine).

Hold it here, breathe in, raise one arm and bring it next to ear.

Breathe out and release.

(You can also hold this position for 10 breaths.)

Repeat 10X

CROSS OVER ON BACK

Rest with upper and mid back on ball.

Lift buttocks until low back flat (neutral spine).

Hold it here, breathe in, raise one arm and straighten out opposite leg.

Breathe out and release.

(You can also hold this position for 10 breaths.)

Repeat 10X

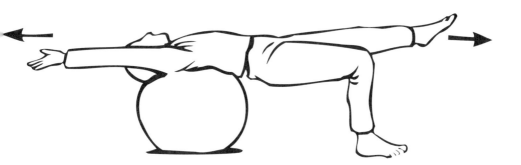

SIDE STRETCH

Rest with your side on ball, lower arm wrapped around ball, upper arm on hip. Lower knee bent.
Breathe in and stretch upper arm over your head.
Hold for five breaths.

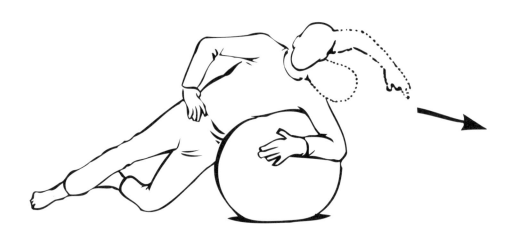

CHAPTER 8

GOLF FITNESS DRILLS
"ON AND OFF THE COURSE"

INTRODUCTION

MUSCLE MEMORY

I called these "On and Off the Course Drills" because one of the most neglected opportunities to do your limbering is "on the course" between shots, on the tee box, before your game. Also, do these anywhere – at home, office, in parking lots, etc. The more **often** you do these drills – **not** the harder you do them – the better you will feel.

Also remember the 7 positions of the **perfect golf swing.** Take a club and practice each of these positions. The more often you get into them and hold each position, the more familiar they will feel doing the swing. It will help to get the feel of the flow. We call this a neurological pattern **or muscle memory.**

DRILLS

#1 FLAT BACK STRETCH

Hold your hands on the top of your club, bend forward,
bending your knees as necessary.
Then push your hands and buttocks away from each other.

Breathe 5X   Come up while bending your knees.

NOTES

#1 SQUAT WITH CLUB

Start as Drill #1, but now bend your knees as much as you can without hurting your knees.

Then push your hands away from your head.

Breathe 5X

NOTES

#3 CHEST AND SHOULDER STRETCH

Pick up club with both hands straight above your head, tuck your buttocks under and hold your belly strong,

Now slowly push your straight arms backward.

Breathe 5X

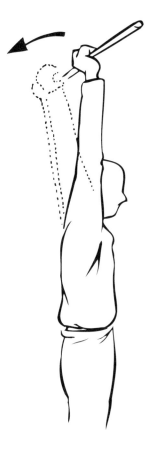

NOTES

#4 ARM SWING STAND UP

Bend forward and squat down; tuck your head under
while you bring your arms behind you. Breathe out
completely!

Breathe in; bringing your arms forward, raising your
head; then, bring the arms up all the way and stand
up, breathing in.

Then squat down again.

Repeat 5X

STAND
UP

NOTES

#5 TORSO TWIST

Hold your club behind your back with your elbows. Take your feet apart 1 foot, bend knees slightly. Now turn your trunk to the right , keeping your hips pointing straight forward! Breathe out as you turn. Then turn trunk to other side.

Repeat 5X

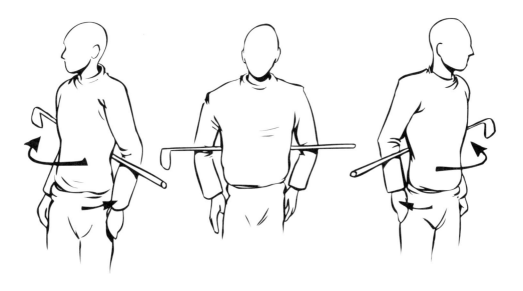

NOTES

#6 SHOULDER SIDE STRETCH

Pick up club with both hands straight above your head, tuck your buttocks under and hold your belly strong.

Pull your right arm up, while pulling your left arm to the left side.

Breathe 5X

NOTES

CHAPTER 9

GOLF FITNESS TOOLS

EQUIPMENT TO ENHANCE
YOUR EXERCISE AND STRETCHING PROGRAM

Here is a list of products no golfer should be without. I picked these because they are easy to use, inexpensive, and deliver big results. I use these frequently with my patients. Beware of exercise items that will be too complex, difficult and expensive . . . they'll soon be gathering dust in your closet! We carry them in the office and they can be ordered through our web site, www.golfhealth.com.

Remember: Exercises only work for you when you do them.

GOLF-Stretch Ball

Big stretch balls have been around for about 60 years and are a great tool. The ball offers a fantastic surface for a multitude of stretches and resistive strengthening exercises. I like these so much that I have included golf-specific stretches and exercises with the Ball in this book. I even bring them to our golf schools. I have students hit a few balls right after doing some of these stretches and they really notice an immediate difference.

GOLF-FlexBand

The GOLF-FlexBand utilizes resistive rubber tubing, which is extremely versatile. It gives you a progressive resistance that eliminates the initial jerking motion we experience with weights. It's much easier on our muscles and ligaments. The GOLF-FlexBand comes in its own pouch with a set of golf-specific exercises for the particular problem area that you have identified with the evaluation. It also helps with neurological patterns, muscle memory and therefore helps training your swing sequence.

Swing Weight

One of the best tools for training your golf swing is a little weighted rubber donut that slips over your club. By putting additional weight on the end of your club, you enhance the feel of the club-head plane. Afterwards, when you swing the club without the weight, your club – and swing – should feel light and easy.

Gyro Hand Exerciser and Power Putty

Both items are extremely effective for increasing your forearm strength. The stronger your forearms are, the lighter you can grip your club as you complete your pendulum motion.

Magnets

Eastern medicine is largely rooted in the belief that energies flow through the muscle tissues. In order to be healthy, the energies (positive and negative) must be held in balance. Magnets produce microcurrents and are believed to aid in creating normal electric current in tissues. Pain causes an electrical disturbance or imbalance that magnets can help by reducing or removing that disturbance.

Topical Lotions

SCI Healthcare Deep Relief System is absolutely the best topical pain relief that I have come across. It has been tested and approved by the PGA Partners Club Test Program and is endorsed and used by a number of professional athletes. The system consists of two lotions – one heating, one cooling. You use them according to what kind of pain you are experiencing, acute or chronic.

Deep Relief Warmth provides fast penetrating warmth that reaches down to sore, aching tissues for immediate pain relief that last for hours.

Deep Relief Cool has a penetrating cooling effect on inflamed tissues. It is great before and after golf to reduce residual muscle soreness.

By mixing the warm and cool products you can adjust the degree of warmth or coolness to your needs. This product line is a must for anybody experiencing soreness or pain from playing golf.

CHAPTER 10

GOLF FITNESS FINAL THOUGHTS

FINAL THOUGHTS

Congratulations!

Finishing your evaluation just put you on your way to playing better golf.

You now have a very good idea of

1 **What your body must do** to have a predictable, efficient golf swing.

2 **What is interfering** with that . . .

3 **How to fix it** and . . .

4 **Some tools** that will help you to accomplish the above.

Now it is time to do the work.

The more consistently you follow these instructions, the faster you will improve your scores and the sooner you will *play golf pain free.*

Now, Go and Enjoy!

PROFESSIONAL TESTIMONIALS

MAURY DEMOTS, GOLF PRO, RIVIERA COUNTRY CLUB
"Full of valuable golf information."

BOB CISCO, PGA CLASS A INSTRUCTOR, RADIO HOST *ALL ABOUT GOLF,* AUTHOR OF *THE ULTIMATE GAME OF GOLF* AND *ULTIMATE PUTTING*
"It's great to teach the golf schools with Dr. Reichardt."

MIKE PERRRYMAN, GOLF PRO, NIKE TOUR
"the missing link in golf education."

TED OH, GOLF PRO, ASIAN TOUR
"I've never felt better...finally my pain is gone."

TESTIMONIALS OF SCHOOL PARTICIPANTS

DAVE GONZALES, *"I have a lower back problem and the exercises helped a lot. I had a much more fluid swing after the exercises ."*

MAX LIPHART, *"The exercises felt challenging because of my preexisting lower back problems. I was able to stretch those muscles I have problems with. After the exercise program I had a better range of motion and better twisting in my upper body."*

BEN DAVIS, FORMER PRO BASKETBALL PLAYER
"The exercises loosened me up and made me feel much more relaxed and not as rigid as before. After the program my golf swing felt more natural and easier without even thinking about it."